Trash and Treasure

Story by Pamela Rushby
Illustrations by Suzie Byrne

ℰHarcourt Achieve

Rigby • Steck-Vaughn

www.HarcourtAchieve.com
1.800.531.5015

Rigby PM Extensions Chapter Books
part of the Rigby PM Program
Emerald Level

Published by Harcourt Achieve Inc.
P.O. Box 26015, Austin, Texas 78755.

U.S. edition © 2004 Harcourt Achieve Inc.

First published in 2003 by Thomson Learning Australia
Trash and Treasure Text © Thomson Learning Australia 2003
Illustrations © Thomson Learning Australia 2003

10 9 8 7 6 5 4 3 2
09

Printed in China by 1010 Printing Limited

Trash and Treasure
ISBN 0 7578 9362 7

Contents

CHAPTER 1

Luck of the Draw

My class was pretty disappointed when we were assigned the Trash and Treasure booth at the school fair.

"Trash!" I said. "Treasure! Why couldn't we have the Chocolate Wheel? Or the Bowling Game? Or the Dunk-the-Principal?"

Our teacher, Mr. Lee, shook his head. "It was absolutely fair, Jon," he said. "The principal pulled classes out of one hat and booths out of another hat. We got the Trash and Treasure booth. That's the way it is. So now … " He paused dramatically. "Guess what?"

"What?" we asked suspiciously.

"Now we are going to run the biggest and best Trash and Treasure booth this school has ever seen!" said Mr. Lee. "Aren't we?"

"S'pose so, sir," we muttered.

"I can't hear you," said Mr. Lee. "The biggest and best. Aren't we?"

We knew what we had to do. "Yes, sir!" we all yelled. "The biggest and best!"

And then, of course, we had to.

We all had to think of ways we could get people to give us a lot of trash and treasure for our booth.

Sam said we could make flyers to put in mailboxes on our streets. The flyers would tell people about the school fair and our booth, and say that we'd be along on Saturday to collect anything they could donate.

"That way, they'll have time to look for lots of things to give us," said Sam.

We all thought that was a good idea.

Laura suggested that we make the collection day a lot of fun.

"We could collect the stuff in wheelbarrows, strollers, and wagons," she said. "We should decorate them with streamers and balloons and tell people when the fair is. Then maybe they'll all come to the fair and buy our stuff."

We thought that was a good idea, too — especially Mr. Lee. "I had no idea I had such a class of entrepreneurs!" he said.

Then he made us go and look up *entrepreneur* in the dictionary.

Weird and Wonderful

We all made flyers about the collection day, and after school we put them into mailboxes.

Then the big collection day arrived. We wondered what we would get. We wondered if we'd get very much at all.

Our parents came with us to help. We pushed our decorated wheelbarrows, strollers, and wagons along the streets. Katy's dad brought his truck, which was great for the bigger things. Katy had even decorated the truck!

People laughed when they saw us, and a lot of them took another look in their garages and sheds to see if they could find anything else for us.

We couldn't believe what people had stored away.

We got some weird things, and we got some wonderful things.

Katy got 15 pairs of rubber boots.

Sam got a baby buggy.

Laura got a bagful of videos from the video store.

Tom got a small TV that almost worked.

We got books and clothes and kitchen pots and pans and flowerpots and a birdcage and a lawnmower.

And I got ... an old sweater.

CHAPTER 3

Helping Mrs. Cesinski

I got the sweater from Mrs. Cesinski. She lives in a very small house on our street, at the top of the hill. She used to live there with Mr. Cesinski, but he died about a year ago.

A few weeks after Mr. Cesinski died, I noticed that Mrs. Cesinski's garbage can wasn't being taken in after garbage day. It was left standing in the street. And the grass in the front yard was getting very long.

I told Mom about it.

"I've noticed that, too," Mom said. "Maybe we should go and visit Mrs. Cesinski."

We walked up the hill, in through Mrs. Cesinski's gate, and up the steps to the front door. Mom knocked. After a little while, we heard Mrs. Cesinski's old dog barking inside. Then we heard someone coming slowly to the door.

Mrs. Cesinski opened the door. Inside the small hall I could see a row of pegs on the wall, with hats and coats hanging on them.

Mrs. Cesinski invited us in. She and Mom sat at the kitchen table and had a cup of tea and talked while I went outside with the old dog. He liked the company, but he was too old and didn't want to play.

I noticed that the grass in the backyard was long, too.

When I came back inside, Mom said, "Jon, it'd be a big help to Mrs. Cesinski if you could take her garbage can in and out for her on garbage days."

"I could do that," I said. "And I could cut the grass too, if you like."

"That's very kind of you, Jon," said Mrs. Cesinski. "I don't like leaving the can on the street, but it's just too hard for me to pull it up the steps. And the mower's very hard for me to push."

After we left, Mom told me that Mrs. Cesinski had wanted to pay me for taking care of the can and the grass. "But I don't think she has much money," Mom said.

"I don't mind doing it," I said. "I don't need to be paid."

"Well, that's nice of you," said Mom. "It's all right to have a drink or a cookie, of course, if you're offered one."

I started taking Mrs. Cesinski's can in and out and mowed the grass every couple of weeks—and I did get offered a drink and a cookie. Not just a cookie, either. Mrs. Cesinski always had hot scones, or a sponge cake, or chocolate chip cookies for me.

"You're a great cook, Mrs. Cesinski!"
I said.

Mrs. Cesinski smiled. "It's nice to
have someone to cook for, Jon," she said.

CHAPTER 4

The Sweater

On our trash and treasure collection day, I almost didn't go to Mrs. Cesinski's house. She wasn't very well off, and I didn't think she'd have anything to give us. But Mom said she might be hurt if I didn't ask her because I'd asked everyone else on the street. So I went.

Mrs. Cesinski smiled when she opened the door. "Hello, Jon!" she said. "What can I do for you, dear?"

I explained what we were doing.

Mrs. Cesinski looked worried. She thought for a moment. "I remember getting the flyer," she said. "But I don't know . . . I would like to give you something, but I don't think I have anything . . ."

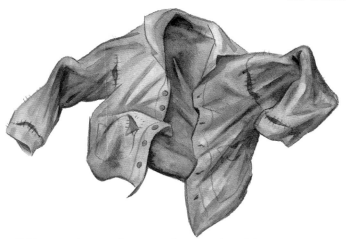

Then her face cleared. She reached up and took something off the row of pegs in the hall. She held it out to me. It was a sweater; a man's sweater. It was very well worn and a bit out of shape.

"Will this do?" she said.

"Thank you," I said politely. "Thank you very much."

I reached out for the sweater. Mrs. Cesinski held onto it for a moment —it was almost as if she didn't want to give it to me. Then she gave it a little stroke and handed it over.

When I showed it to Mom she said, "I suppose it used to be her husband's. It's rather old, isn't it? I wonder if it will sell?"

CHAPTER 5

Trash?

The kids at school didn't think it would sell at all.

"Too old. Too ratty," they said. "We've got a lot of treasure. That's definitely part of the trash!"

Some of them thought it was a waste of time putting it in the booth at all. "No one will want it," they said.

But Mr. Lee said to put it in the booth. "If Mrs. Cesinski was kind enough to give it to us, the least we can do is put it out," he said. "It might be just what someone wants."

But the sweater didn't seem to be the sort of thing anybody would want.

On the day of the fair our Trash and Treasure booth was a big success. We sold the boots—all 15 pairs of them. The baby buggy and the lawnmower went in the first five minutes. We sold the videos, the birdcage, the books, the clothes, the pots and pans, and even the small TV that almost worked.

Toward the end of the afternoon, there were only a few things left in our booth. Things that were there were definitely trash. And one of them was Mrs. Cesinski's sweater.

It was getting late. We were talking about packing up when Katy gave me a sharp nudge.

"Look!" she said. "Look who's coming!"

"Who?" I asked.

"Mrs. Cesinski!" hissed Katy.

I looked at the sweater lying in the nearly empty booth with a few leftover pieces of unwanted trash. There was a doll with no arms, a chipped garden gnome, a pile of old car magazines, and Mrs. Cesinski's sweater.

I watched Mrs. Cesinski getting closer and closer.

"Hide the sweater!" I said. "Hide it, quick!" I didn't want Mrs. Cesinski to think the sweater she'd given us was trash.

But it was too late. Mrs. Cesinski was standing right in front of us. I tried as hard as I could to stand between Mrs. Cesinski and the sweater. I hoped she wouldn't see it. It almost worked.

"Hello, Jon," Mrs. Cesinski said. "I thought I'd come and see if I could buy something from your booth."

She looked over the booth, which was nearly empty.

"It looks as if I've come a bit late," she said. "There's almost nothing left. You have done well!" She looked at the booth again. "I did want to support your booth, but I'm afraid there's really nothing here I'd want ..."

Then her eyes lit up.

"Oh yes!" she said. "Yes! There is something I want!"

And she reached right around me and picked up the sweater.

CHAPTER 6

Treasure

I couldn't believe it!

"But … but … Mrs. Cesinski," I said. "You gave that to us. You didn't want it!"

Mrs. Cesinski wasn't looking at us. She was stroking the sweater, smiling.

"I was wrong," she said. "I do want it. I want it very much. How much is it?"

We didn't want to take any money from Mrs. Cesinski. It seemed wrong, making her pay for something she'd given to us in the first place. But Mrs. Cesinski insisted.

Then Katy tried to put the sweater into a bag for her, but Mrs. Cesinski wouldn't let her. "I'll carry it, thank you," she said.

We all watched Mrs. Cesinski walk away. She was still stroking the sweater.

"That's really weird," Sam said. "She gave it to us, then she bought it back. Why do you suppose she wanted that piece of trash back?"

The kids all turned away and started to pack up the booth.

Mr. Lee and I watched Mrs. Cesinski walk out of the school grounds. She was hugging the sweater close to her.

"Mrs. Cesinski's sweater wasn't trash at all, was it?" I asked Mr Lee.

He smiled at me. "No, Jon," Mr. Lee said. "I think it was the biggest treasure in our booth."